# What Everybody Should Know About the Jew!

Dr. Aaron B. Claxton

What Everybody Should Know About the Jew!

Copyright © 2018 by Dr. Aaron B. Claxton

All rights reserved. No part of this book may be reproduced or transmitted in any form or by any means without written permission of the author.

Unless otherwise indicated, all Scripture quotations are taken from the King James Version (KJV) of the Holy Bible (public domain).

ISBN: 979-8-8690-0428-4

Published by Kingdom Publishing, LLC
Odenton, Maryland 21113
Printed in the USA

# What Everybody Should Know About the Jew!

The Jewish nation is unique among all the 70 nations of the world (Genesis 10:1-32).

Notice the peculiar statement made of the Jews in Zechariah 8:23. The verse says, "Thus says the LORD of hosts: In those days (the end time days) ten men from every language of the nations shall grasp the corner of the garment of a Jewish man, saying, 'Let us go with you, for we have heard that God is with you.'"

Exodus 19:5 says, "…then you shall be <u>a special treasure to me above all people;</u> for all the earth is Mine." Exodus 19:6 also, says, "And you shall be to me a <u>kingdom of priests</u> and a holy nation." These verses declare that Israel or the Jew would be a special, holy people to Him.  Of all the seventy nations on the earth (Genesis 10:1-31), God chose Israel to be special and the priestly nation unto Him to make atonement and intercession for all of the seventy nations of the earth (Leviticus 23:27-28).

Jehovah chose the children of Israel by His own free will to make them His own peculiar people. Deuteronomy 7:6-8 says, "'For you are a holy people to the LORD your God: the LORD your God has chosen you to be a people for Himself, a special treasure above all the peoples on the face of the earth.

"The LORD did not set His love on you nor choose you because you were in number more than any other people, for you were the least of all other of all peoples; but because the LORD loves you, and because He would keep the oath which He swore to your fathers the LORD has brought you out with a mighty hand."

Let us observe this fact that the Israelites are the most blessed people upon the face of the earth. In Genesis 12:1-3 the LORD speaks a sevenfold blessing upon Abram and his seed, as the LORD spoke to Abram a <u>second time</u> saying, "Now the LORD had said to Abram, 'Get out of your country, from your family and from your father's house to a land I will show you. I will bless you and make you a great nation; I will bless you and make your name great; and you shall be a blessing. I will bless those who bless you, and curse him who curses you: and in you all the families of the earth shall be blessed.'"

Let's continue recording God's blessings on Abram: "then Melchizedek King of Salem (Jerusalem) brought out bread and wine (Bible's first communion); he was priest of God Most High, and he blessed him and said:
"Blessed be Abram of God Most High, possessor (owner) of heaven and earth. And blessed be God Most High, who has delivered your enemies unto your hand (Gen. 14:18-20) and he gave him a tithe of all." In Genesis 15:1, the word of God states, "After all these things the word of the LORD came to Abram in a vision, saying, 'Do not be afraid Abram, I am your shield, your exceeding great reward! And behold, the word of the LORD came to him saying, 'this one (Eliezer of Damascus) shall not be your heir but one who will <u>come from your own body</u> shall be your heir (Isaac).'

"Then He said to him!' I am the LORD, who brought you out of Ur of the Chaldeans (Iraq), to give you this land to inherit it… To your descendants I have given this land (the Holy Land) from the river of Egypt (the Nile) to the great river, the river, the River Euphrates" (Genesis 15:1, 18).

Verses 13-14 says, "Then He said to Abram, 'Know certainly that your descendants will be strangers in a land that is not theirs, and will serve them, and they will afflict them four hundred years. And the nation whom they serve I will judge afterward; afterward they shall come out with great possessions."

Deuteronomy Chapter 28 speaks strongly of Jehovah's blessings upon the Israelites. The word says: "Now it shall come to pass if you diligently obey the voice the LORD your God to observe carefully all His commandments which I command you today, that the LORD your God will set thee high above all nations… The LORD will command <u>the blessing</u> on you in your storehouses and in all which you set your hand… you shall lend to many nations, but you shall not borrow! And the LORD will make you the head and not the tail; you shall be above only, and not beneath; if you heed the commandments of the LORD your God..." (Deut. 28:1-13).

It is a historical fact that Jews have been awarded Nobel Peace Prizes more than any nationality of people on the face of the earth! Mark Zuckerberg who invented Facebook is a Jew and a billionaire!

Hitler was jealous of and hated the Jews because they were so blessed. He called them the "merchant class" who would take over the finances of the world if not stopped!

God ordained that every Israelite should be able to read. Therefore, He gave them <u>ten</u> brief commandments. Other nations like Egypt and Babylon had codes consisting of thousands of hieroglyphics that only special classes of professionals could decipher. In those nations the common people were illiterate; they could not read.

The Israelites were controlled by God's law and their inner conscience.

The Jews historically have been the most important people upon the earth. Their law and their obedience to same shined a light of the will of God to all the other nations of the world.

This priestly, intercessory nation of people were and are a blessing to all nations of the earth. They only have meant good for the other nations. However, Satan's jealousy and hatred of them has moved him to harm and persecute Jews throughout the history of the human race.

The Prophet Isaiah wrote concerning the last days:

"Now it shall come to pass in the latter days that the mountain of the LORD'S house shall be established on the top of the mountains. And shall be exalted above the hills; and <u>all nations</u> shall flow to it. Many people shall come and say, 'Come, and let us go up to the mountain of the LORD, to the house of the God of Jacob.

"He will teach us His ways, and we shall walk in His paths; For out of Zion shall go forth the law, And that the word of the LORD from Jerusalem…

O house of Jacob, come and let us walk in the light of the LORD" (Isaiah 2:2-3, 5).

As we continue with the book, "WHAT EVERYONE SHOULD KNOW ABOUT THE JEW," the Prophet Zechariah wrote:

"But now I will not treat the remnant of this people as in the former days, 'Says the LORD of hosts, for the seed shall be prosperous. The vine shall give its fruit, the ground shall give her increase, and the heavens shall give dew-I will cause the remnant of this people to possess these, and it shall come to pass…O house of Judah and house of Israel, I will save you, and you shall be a blessing. Do not fear. Do not fear, Let your hands be strong" (Zechariah 8:11-13).

Thus you have seen from many biblical references that the Israelites and the Jews are indeed God's chosen, handpicked and special people. As you are aware, within the past few days, our President, Donald Trump, has declared that <u>Jerusalem</u> is in fact the historic capital of Israel.

Zechariah goes on to say, "Let us continue to go and <u>pray</u> before the LORD, and seek the LORD of hosts. I myself will go also. Yes, many peoples and strong nations shall come to see the LORD of hosts <u>in Jerusalem</u> and pray before the LORD."

We repeat from the beginning of this book, "Thus says the LORD of hosts;" in those days (these last days) ten men from every language of the nations shall grasp the sleeve (the helm) of a Jewish man, saying, 'Let us go with you, for we have heard that God is with you'" (Zechariah 8:12-22).

By now, you should be totally convinced that the seed of Abraham, the Israelites are God's chosen people of all the nations upon the face of the earth. We Christians ought to know that we too are the seed of Abraham, and all the blessings and benefits that accrue unto them, belong to us also!

The Apostle Paul wrote in the book of Romans the following:

"For if the first fruits are holy, the lump is also holy; and if the root is holy, so are the branches. And if some of the branches were broken off, and you (Gentiles) being a wild olive tree were grafted in among them, and with them became a <u>partaker of the root and fatness</u> of the olive tree" (Romans 11:16-17).

The Apostle Paul put in another way,

"The Scripture, foreseeing that God would justify the Gentiles by faith, preached the gospel to Abraham beforehand saying, 'In you all the nations shall be blessed. So then those who are of faith are blessed with believing Abraham…Christ has redeemed us from the curse of the law, having become a curse for us (for it is written,) 'Cursed is everyone who hangs on a tree' that the blessing of Abraham (righteousness by faith) might come on the Gentiles in Christ Jesus, that we might receive the promise of the Spirit through faith. But after faith has come, we (the Jews) are no longer under the law. For you are <u>all sons of God through faith in Jesus Christ</u>…And if you are Christ's then <u>are you Abraham's seed, and heirs</u> according to the promise" (Galatians 3:8-29).

Paul expands on this truth and revelation to the saints at Ephesus. Here he says: "Therefore remember that you, once Gentiles in the flesh-who are called Uncircumcision by what is called the Circumcision made in the flesh by hands…But now in Christ Jesus you who were afar off have been brought near by the blood of Christ. For He Himself is our peace who made <u>both</u> (Jew and Gentile) <u>one</u>, and has broken down the middle wall of separation… so as to create in Himself <u>one new man from the two</u> thus making peace…and came and preached peace to you who were afar off and to those who were near; for through Him we both (Jew and Gentile) have access by one Spirit to the Father."

"Now therefore, you (Gentiles) are no longer strangers and foreigners, but fellow citizens with the saints (the Jews) and members of the household of God" (Ephesians 2:11-19).

So there you have it. The Church is made-up of former Jews and Gentiles, and we are now one people in Christ! We both will suffer the horrors of the great tribulation or the "time of Jacob's trouble" (Daniel 12:7). When Christ returns in His Second Coming (or the Rapture) He will unite and glorify His Body – the Church, which is also His Bride – in the midair and continue His descent to the earth when His feet will land on the Mount of Olives; from which He will fight with and destroy His enemies and establish His earthy Kingdom.

Zechariah wrote, "Behold, the day of the LORD is coming…Then the LORD will go forth and fight against those nations. As He fights in the day of battle, And in that day His feet will stand on the Mount of Olives…Thus the LORD my God will come and all the saints with Him… And the LORD shall be King over all the earth" (Zechariah 14:3-9).

The Apostle Jude puts it this way: "Behold the LORD comes with ten thousands of His saints (the Church, the One New Man) to execute judgement on all, to convict all who are ungodly among them of all their ungodly deeds, which they have committed in an ungodly way and of all the harsh things which ungodly sinners have spoken against Him" (Jude 1:14-15).

Thus you have the story of "What Everybody Should Know About The Jew"!

## ABOUT THE AUTHOR

Dr. Aaron B. Claxton has been in Christ for nearly 60 years and has preached the gospel for nearly 60 years.

Dr. Claxton is the father of seven children. A precious firstborn daughter, Gayle.

He has been married to his lovely wife, Deborah, for nearly 60 years. They are the proud parents of six children (four boys and two girls), all have been called into the five-fold ministry. The Claxtons are also blessed with a host of grandchildren, great grandchildren and 1 great-great grandchild.

Dr. Claxton's academic background includes earned degrees from Morgan State University, from the Mount Royal College of the Bible and from St. Mary's Seminary and University, where he pursued the academics for the Doctor of Ministry degree. He completed that degree in 1996 at the Family Bible Seminary. Dr. Claxton has been awarded two honorary Doctorate degrees from Christian International University. They are the Doctor of Divinity and the Doctor of Laws degrees. He received his PhD degree in Biblical Studies from Family Bible Seminary in May 2003.

Apostle Claxton, along with his wife, Deborah, founded and pastored the New Creation Christian Church in Baltimore, Maryland for twenty-three years. He has taught at three Bible Colleges and is well traveled, having preached the Gospel across America and in sixteen nations around the world.

Dr. Claxton stands in the office of Apostle, formally overseeing one hundred plus churches in the U.S., and in East and West Africa and is presently being established in a global, apostolic ministry, along with his wife, Deborah in her apostolic ministry. His oldest son, Apostle Aaron Bryan Claxton, along with his wife, Sheila, now pastor the headquarters church in Baltimore, which Dr. Claxton founded in 1968.

MORE BOOKS BY DR. AARON B. CLAXTON

In addition to this prolific masterpiece, Dr. Claxton has authored over thirty books of which twelve (12) are published:

- God's Plan for the Sons of Ham – *a Future and a Hope*

- The Biblical View of the Rapture and the Second Coming

- Farrakhan, Islam and Jesus the Messiah

- The Blessing of the Lord is Upon the Tither

- First Fruits the Missing Offering

- Possessing Our Earthly Inheritance **Now!**

- Caught Up to Meet Him

- Understanding the Root, the Causes and the Remedy
  of the Middle East Conflict

- ISIS: The Church's Wake Up Call

- Unveiling the Truth About the War in the Womb

- Beloved, Let's Get the Rapture Right!
- Beyond Sodom: Has America Lost God's Smiles?

# Two other books by the author related to this subject:

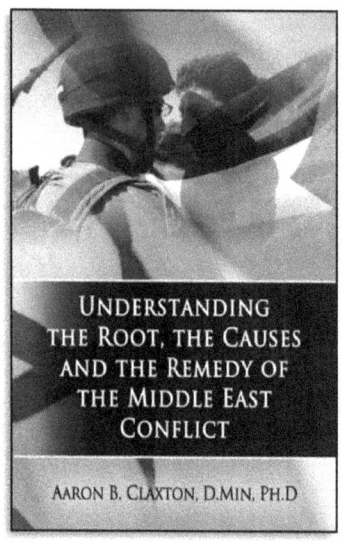

### Understanding the Root, the Causes and the Remedy of the Middle East Conflict

The Brief study in this book will acquaint the reader with the biblical, ethnic, historical and geographical roots of the age-long struggles between the seed of Ishmael and the seed of Isaac concerning who is the rightful owner of the 'holy land.'

Ishmael was Abraham's firstborn son by his Egyptian handmaid, Hagar. Isaac was Abraham's long-awaited son by his wife, Sarah called, 'the son of promise.'

It was God Almighty who chose Isaac over Ishmael and gave Isaac and his seed a divine land grant consisting of all the land from Lebanon to the Euphrates (Iraq).

A long scenario of events transpired to eventually see Isaac's seed cast out of the land in 721 B.C., and finally in 70 A.D.

As far back as Moses, the Lord warned the children of Israel against idolatry and the consequences of being scattered from the land. In the latter days they would repent, turn back to God and be restored back into their covenant land and to God (Deut. 4:25-31).

Ishmael's seed, the present-day Muslims, have strongly felt for ages that the land belongs to them. They hate the Jews. Thus, we see the age-long conflict of the 'holy land.'

Unveiling the Truth About the War in the Womb

The essential story about the mystery of the "War in the Womb" is recorded in Genesis 25:21-23. The word of God says,

"Now Isaac pleaded with the Lord for his wife, because she was barren; and the Lord granted his plea and Rebekah his wife conceived. But the children struggled together within her; and she said, 'If all is well, why am I like this?' So, she went to inquire of the Lord.

"And the Lord said to her: 'Two nations are in your womb, Two peoples shall be separated from your body, one people shall be stronger than the other, and the older shall serve the younger.'"

The name of these twin brothers are Esau and Jacob - Esau the elder twin came out first and Jacob the younger brother caught hold of Esau's heel. Esau's name means "hairy" or "red" and Jacob's name means "Supplanter" or "Deceiver."

The long and short of this story is that God chose Jacob (Israel) over Esau. Jacob became the father of the Israelite nation while Esau became one of the founders of the Arabic nation which subsequently became the Muslim people. The war that began in the womb continues until today.

The conclusion of this war will be wrought by the Lord Jesus Christ at His Second Coming! (Isaiah 63:1-9 and Obadiah Chapter 1).

# Book Dr. Deborah Claxton

## The Wonders of Widowhood

This book will help you to see Widowhood like you have never seen it before. Dr. Deborah not only shares her experiences since becoming a widow in November 2018 but digs unto God's mandates concerning them. She discusses the plight of widowhood and how it is to be addressed. You will be amazed as you discover the premium that God places upon widowhood. Also, what He says concerning those who misuse and abuse them.

Read about how Jesus treated widows when he encountered them throughout his earthly ministry. Similarly, there are insightful stories about various widows mentioned in the Bible.

This book is not only a "must read" for the widow or widower, but has a message for singles, married couples, divorcees, and anyone who wants to learn more about the love of God toward all humanity.

In addition, there are some valuable insights shared by other widows and widowers as they traversed their painful encounter with spousal transition.

The author has also included some of her poems written during her alone time with her creator and friend - The Lord who is her "Husband". (Isa.54:5)

## NEW CREATION CHRISTIAN CHURCH

New Creation is a local non-denominational Christian church with a Kingdom global perspective. We are intimate enough to get to know you and your family, and large enough to impact the Greater Baltimore community, the nation, and the world.

*"Changing Lives Through Christ"*

Contact us: www.NewCreation-MD.org or (410) 488-5650

Email us: info@ncccbalto.org

Address: 5401 Frankford Ave, Baltimore, MD, United States, 21206

Live Streaming:

    facebook.com/NCCCBaltimoreMD

    Instagram.com/NCCCBaltimoreMD

    youtube.com/@newcreationchristianchurch280

www.ingramcontent.com/pod-product-compliance
Lightning Source LLC
LaVergne TN
LVHW061044070526
838201LV00073B/5169